The *GOLF Magazine*

Full Swing

Handbook

Other titles in the series

The *GOLF Magazine* Golf Fitness Handbook
The *GOLF Magazine* Mental Golf Handbook
The *GOLF Magazine* Course Management Handbook
The *GOLF Magazine* Short Game Handbook
The *GOLF Magazine* Putting Handbook

The *GOLF Magazine*
Full Swing
Handbook

Peter Morrice
and the Editors of *GOLF Magazine*

Photography by Sam Greenwood

The Lyons Press

First Lyons Press edition, 2000

Printed in the United States of America
Design and composition by Compset, Inc.

10 9 8 7 6 5 4 3 2 1

The Library of Congress Cataloging-in-Publication Data

Morrice, Peter.
    The Golf magazine full swing handbook/Peter
Morrice and the editors of Golf magazine; illustrated
by Sam Greenwood.—1st Lyons Press ed.
        p. cm.
    ISBN: 1–55821–937–4
    1. Swing (Golf)—Handbooks, manuals, etc.
    I. Title: Full swing handbook. II. Title.

GV979.S9 M67 2000
796.352'3—dc21

                                        99-086540

Photography on page 20 copyright © Fred Vuich

Acknowledgments

Many people contributed to the making of this book. First, my gratitude to George Peper, editor-in-chief of *GOLF Magazine*, who trusted this project in my hands. And to Bryan Oettel and Jill Hindle at The Lyons Press, whose editorial skills and professionalism made them perfect partners. For the photographs, I thank *GOLF Magazine* staff photographer Sam Greenwood, as well as Mike Stubblefield, Dennis Blake, Mike LaBrutto, and Wendy Obenrader, who modeled for and helped with the photo shoots. Lastly, a big thanks to my family and friends for their patience and constant encouragement during late nights and long weekends. Special recognition goes to my parents: my father for the golf, my mother for the writing.

Contents

Foreword

At *GOLF Magazine* we use two methods to determine the content to include each month: surveys and guts. In the survey method, questionnaires are sent to thousands of our subscribers, asking what topics they enjoy most, which kinds of articles they prefer, etc. In the guts method, we editors simply use our intuition as kindred, hopelessly addicted golfers.

But no matter which method we use, the number-one answer is always the same: instruction. "Give us more instruction," has been the mandate from our readers ever since the magazine began publishing forty years ago. The reason is simple: A golfer is happiest when his game is improving.

Recently, however, we've learned a couple of things about how to present our instruction. Number one, you like it short and sweet. After all, most of the current populace was raised on television, sound bites, and quick delivery of information, from beepers to e-mail. More than ever, we like our messages short and to the point.

And the "to the point" part is just as important as the "short" part. For the last decade or so, the most popular portion of GOLF Magazine has been the buff-colored section called "Private Lessons," which brings together custom-tailored instruction for five different kinds of golfers: low handicappers, high handicappers, short but straight hitters, long but crooked hitters, and senior golfers. In this way, we're able to speak more personally to our readers and help them more individually with their games.

Why am I telling you all this? Because the same kind of thinking went into the book that is now in your hands. When the people at The Lyons Press came to talk to us about a partnership in golf book publishing, we gave them our mantra for success: instruction, succinct and focused. The result is the GOLF Magazine series of guides, each written concisely, edited mercilessly, and dedicated entirely to one key aspect of playing the game.

Each *GOLF Magazine* guide assembles a wealth of great advice in a package small enough to carry in your golf bag. We hope you'll use these pages to raise your game to a whole new level.

George Peper
Editor-in-Chief
GOLF Magazine

The *GOLF Magazine*
Full Swing
Handbook

Introduction

It's hitting that career drive or nipping a long iron off the fairway. It's watching an approach shot climb with a slight draw, float over the pin, and pull up next to the hole. The object of golf may be to make the lowest score, but these are the things that make golfers tick. You may respect the guy who sprays it all over but manages decent scores, but the player who bombs it off the tee and attacks the pins . . . he's the golfer you want to be.

Not to knock the short game. It's well established that some 60 percent of the average player's score comes within 100 yards of the hole. That said, if you want to see your scores come down, grab your wedges and your putter and go to work on the short stuff. But that's like being told to eat your vegetables: You know it's good advice but you just can't get yourself to do it.

Simply put, the long game is too tantalizing to pass up. Watching a well-struck ball soar through the air has an intoxicating effect on golfers. That's why they spend their practice hours at the driving range instead of the putting green. Hitting balls is entertainment; practicing putting for any length of time feels like solitary confinement. And while a better short game may be the quickest way to lower your scores, this book presumes that golf is more to you than just posting a number.

In the pages that follow, we'll pull apart the golf swing and tell you what has to happen and why, but first we'll take a detailed look at the setup. To put it bluntly, you simply cannot be an effective golfer without solid, consistent address positions. Truth is, much of your performance is predetermined before you even take the club back by the angles and positions you create at address. Physics tells us that.

Once we get the setup down, we'll start on the swing itself, from the takeaway to the finish, in simple, understandable terms. No bizarre ideas or unproven theories here, just the time-tested, mainstream teachings that the world's best teachers and players have relied on for years. With an understanding of the basic parts of the swing, you can learn how to blend them together into a cohesive, effective swing motion.

Our next step will be to define common problems, such as slicing, hitting fat, and topping, and discuss what causes them. As random as they may seem, all bad shots have a logical explanation. We'll take a brief look at how the most common come to be, and then we'll finish up with a section on how to get the most out of your practice time.

Throughout the book, you'll also find a recurring feature called "Best Tip," a sampling of the greatest tips ever published in *GOLF Magazine*. Most of this instruction comes from *GOLF Magazine*'s Top 100 Teachers, the industry's definitive collection of swing doctors. We dispense their ideas in every issue of the magazine, and here you'll enjoy some of their best full-swing tips and drills in a single volume.

Whether you're a newcomer to golf, a frustrated middle handicapper, or a hotshot looking to take your game to the next level, this book will provide you with a brief yet comprehensive look at the fundamentals of the swing. With a little dedication and a well-formed improvement plan, you can become the player you dream of being. Let's get started.

Preswing

Next time you go to the driving range, take a look at the folks around you. Chances are, you'll be standing in the midst of middle-handicap America. Ask around and you'll find they're trying to fix their slice, get more distance, hit the ball higher, and so on. All noble intentions, but most golfers think they'll naturally groove a better swing simply by hitting ball after ball until their hands throb. In the end, all they get is tired.

Now compare this scene of panting, ball-beating middle handicappers to the practice area at a professional tour event. If you've never been to one, trust me when I tell you the pros hit balls about half as fast as amateurs do. And what are most of them focusing on? Preswing fundamentals. Things

Tour pros work long hours on perfecting their setup.

like alignment and ball position and posture. They know that how they set up either promotes or prevents the right positions during the swing. They also know it's a lot easier to monitor and change static positions than swing positions.

You may find it amazing that the world's best players work on simple things that many amateurs think they had figured out years ago, but it's true. Every day the pros go back to the basics, knowing these are the building blocks of the golf swing. Let that be a revelation to you.

Jack Nicklaus, in his instruction manual *Golf My Way* wrote, "I think it [the setup] is the single most important maneuver in golf. . . . If you set up correctly, there's a good chance you'll hit a reasonable shot, even if you make a mediocre swing. If you set up incorrectly, you'll hit a lousy shot even if you make the greatest swing in the world." Actually, you *need* to make a faulty swing if it starts from a faulty setup. In effect, by making errors at address you require in-swing errors to compensate for them.

So, put aside that feeling that you already know how to set up to a golf ball. If you'd like to play better, do what the pros do and perfect your address positions. It's the only logical place to start.

The Grip

If you're like most golfers, the last thing you want to hear is that you have to change your grip. Golf is a humbling game in which you're constantly trying to assert control yet often feel like you have none. Your grip is your one connection to the golf club, and whether it's good or bad, it's yours. You rely on it for a sense of control, and no golfer wants to give that up.

But before you dismiss the idea of changing your grip, answer this: Would you like to get rid of that slice of yours? How about hitting the ball another 20 yards? Ahhh, now I've got your attention. Fact is, how you grip the club at address in large part determines the position of the clubface at impact, which plays a major role in the direction of your shots. The grip also figures prominently in how much power you can produce during the swing. In short, if you care about how far and how straight you hit the ball, you need to care about your grip.

Hitting It Straight

The way you grip the club influences how the clubface rotates during the swing—from open to square to closed like a swinging door. And the position of the clubface at impact dictates how the ball will curve in the air. For example, if the clubface is angled to the right, or "open," when it contacts the ball, the ball will pick up left-to-right sidespin and curve to the right. If the clubface is angled to the left, or "closed," the ball will take on right-to-left sidespin and curve left. It's that simple: The squareness of the clubface when it meets the ball is the only factor that affects the curvature of the shot.

But how does the way you grip the club affect clubface position at impact? Consider this: Your hands are pulled into certain positions on the downswing by the centrifugal force of the swing, like they would be in a game of tug-of-war. Let's call these "natural positions." If the hands don't match these natural positions at address, the clubface will either open or close when the hands assume these positions on the downswing.

The natural position for your left hand is however it hangs at your side; this is how it will return to the ball at impact. The position of your right hand is a different story, as the right hand makes a striking, or spanking, action at impact. To promote this, your right palm should point to the target at address. If your hands start in these positions and your clubface is square to the target, your clubface will return square at impact without manipulation.

Power Is in Your Hands

How does the correct grip promote more power in your swing? Think about what happens to your wrists as you swing back and through: They hinge the club up going back, unhinge coming down, and

Position your left hand on the grip however it naturally hangs at your side.

Your right palm should face the target at address.

then rehinge on the follow-through. Get a club and try it. This may seem like a natural and inconsequential action, but it is a major power generator in the golf swing.

As the wrists hinge going back, they create an angle between the left arm and the club, thereby introducing a second lever to the swing. (The first lever, a straight line from the left shoulder to the clubhead, is established at address.) As wrist hinge produces this second lever, the clubhead can travel through a much longer arc than it could in a single-lever motion. And a longer arc means more room

Proper wrist hinge promotes a full swing arc.

for the clubhead to accelerate on the downswing. Furthermore, as centrifugal force on the downswing unhinges the wrists, pulling the left arm and the club back into a straight line, the clubhead is flung into the ball with great force. That's the whipping action you see in good players.

Believe it or not, the grip is at the root of this wrist action. To understand this, get a club and place the grip diagonally across your left palm, running from your

Handle With Care

Grip thickness is one equipment variable that receives little attention. While standard, off-the-rack grips are fine for many golfers, make sure your grips are right for you. The critical check is in the left hand. Take your normal left-hand grip and check that the tips of your middle two fingers are lightly touching your palm. If the fingertips are either not reaching the palm or digging into it, your grips are the wrong size, which can have a profound effect on how you move the club.

forefinger to your heel pad, and close your fingers around it. Now, with your hand at your side, try to cock the clubhead up in front of you simply by hinging your left wrist. Not easy, right? Now grip the club again, this time holding the handle across the base of your fingers, and try that same exercise. You'll find you can cock the clubhead up farther and with greater ease with the handle in your fingers.

This is precisely how the left wrist should hinge during the golf swing and the reason the handle

The popular Vardon, or overlapping grip.

must be held in the fingers of the left hand. Likewise with the right hand, as the right wrist also must hinge. With the handle placed correctly and the hands in their natural positions on the club, the hands and arms can contribute significant power and also square the clubface at impact.

How to Find Your Best Grip

Let your left hand hang at your side. Your palm probably doesn't directly face your left leg; with most people, it's rotated slightly inward. To demonstrate this, lay a pencil loosely in your fingers and again let your hand hang. Is the pencil sticking straight out? It's likely pointing slightly to the right. This is the natural position of your left hand, a position it will seek out unless forced otherwise, so place your hand like this on the grip.

Generally speaking, the handle should run from the middle of your left forefinger to just under the heel pad of the hand. When you close your fingers around the grip, feel as if you're holding the handle against your palm with your fingers, the butt of the club sitting firmly under the heel pad. Then add the right hand, also setting the handle in the fingers. The visual here is that the right palm should face the target at address, matching the clubface, as it will make a palm-to-target striking action at impact.

As for how to join the hands, most instructors recommend the Vardon, or overlapping, grip, where the little finger of the right hand hooks around the left forefinger. For most golfers, this arrangement offers the best combination of control in the fingers and range of motion in the wrists.

BEST TIP: The Impact Test

Centrifugal force causes the joints of the left wrist, elbow, and shoulder to line up in a certain way at impact. An effective grip delivers a square clubface as this lining up occurs.

You can simulate this pulling force as follows: Grip a 5-iron in your left hand as you normally do and hold the club out in front of you with the toe straight up. Have a friend hook his fingers around the clubhead. Then slowly lean back, letting your body weight straighten out your left arm (see photo at right). This is how your joints will line up at impact. If your grip is good, your clubface will remain square, or toe-up, as you lean back. If the clubhead twists left or right, adjust your left-hand grip accordingly.

—Robert Baker, *GOLF Magazine*
Master Teaching Professional

BEST TIP: Follow the exercise at left to see if your left-hand grip promotes a square clubface at impact.

Tension Control

There are all sorts of images out there for monitoring grip pressure. Sam Snead used to say to pretend you're holding a baby bird, while another image equates grip pressure to squeezing a tube of toothpaste. While these thoughts may be helpful, you alone have to determine how much pressure is right for your swing.

You should feel as though you're gripping as lightly as you can without losing control of the club during the swing. Due to the swing's high velocity, you need a secure hold with your fingers, but you don't want to create undue tension in your wrists and forearms. Setting the handle in your fingers, not your palms, will help keep the wrists and arms relaxed, as flexing the hand muscles sends tension up the arms.

Experiment on the practice tee with different levels of grip pressure. When you find one that seems right for you, rate it on a scale of 1 to 10 (1 being the lightest; 10 the tightest). If your ideal grip is a 5, for instance, make that one of your preswing checkpoints. You'll be amazed how much faster you can swing the club with a lighter grip.

> ### *BEST TIP: The Pincher Drill*
>
> Excessive pressure in the last three fingers of each hand causes the forearms to become rigid. To relieve this tension, make some pitch swings using a "pincher grip," with just the thumb and forefinger of each hand gripping the club and the other six fingers flared out. Notice how well you can control the club with such little grip pressure. Try to incorporate more "pinch pressure" into your normal grip.
>
> —Kip Puterbaugh, *GOLF Magazine*
> Top 100 Teacher

Aim and Alignment

Golf is a game of precision disguised as a walk in the park. Think about it: You stand on most tees and gaze out over a 40-yard-wide target, any part of which you'd be happy to play your next shot from. Then you hit into greens bigger than most backyards—and again, you'll take any shot that ends up on the putting surface. In fact, it seems the only time you have a specific target is when you're putting. And they call this a target sport?

They do, and it most certainly is. However, many golfers get lulled into complacency, even sheer sloppiness, by the apparent size of their targets. They set up to shots as if direction is of little concern, and then can't believe it when their ball sails into trouble. It's crazy: Golfers try so hard to get their swing right so they can hit the ball well, and when they do, it goes in the wrong direction because of careless aim and alignment.

Granted, there are legions of faults that cause shots to fly off-line, but poor aim and alignment are among the biggest culprits. And since they occur before the swing begins, they are the easiest to rectify. Unfortunately, some golfers find the aiming process mundane and therefore disregard it; others fail to appreciate the consequences. Whatever the reason, the golfer who neglects these preshot essentials is leaving his performance up to chance: A perfect swing is wasted if it isn't preceded by good aim and alignment.

A Game of Direction

First, let's get our definitions down. "Aim" refers to the position of the clubface relative to the target, while "alignment" refers to the position of the body relative to the target line—an imaginary line drawn from the ball to the target. It's useful to think of

"Aim" is the angle of the clubface relative to the target.

aiming and aligning as two different actions, because they affect shot direction in different ways.

Aiming sets the clubface at address, which often determines its position at impact and therefore the way the ball curves in the air. But ball flight is a function not only of curvature, but also of the shot's starting direction; this is where alignment enters the picture.

On full shots, the path of the swing primarily determines the ball's starting direction; the momentum of the clubhead propels the ball in whatever direction it's tracking on. This swing direction tends to

Swing path mainly determines a shot's starting direction.

follow the alignment of the body lines—imaginary lines across the feet, knees, hips, and shoulders. Although the body lines tend to line up with one another, the shoulders are the key, since the arms hang directly from the shoulder sockets. So, instead of checking the squareness of your stance to assess alignment, as most golfers do, have a friend hold a club across your shoulders to see where they're pointed; they have the biggest impact on swing path.

I have already touched upon clubface aim and how the grip plays a leading role in the rotation of the clubface during the swing. But the positioning of the clubface at address drives the entire aiming process. If you watch the pros, you'll see they aim the clubface first, then step into their stance and align their body. This order is critical: At address you have a better view of the clubface then you do your various body lines and can therefore aim the face with greater accuracy. Then, a square clubface can serve as a valuable reference point when you align your body.

How to Aim and Align

Should all golfers employ the same aim and alignment? In a perfect world, they would. If the clubface is perfectly square at impact and the clubhead is moving directly along the target line, the result is a shot that flies straight to the target. And straight shots should be preceded by square aim and alignment. However, golfers know such shots are few and far between.

More likely, you get into the habit of aiming and aligning a certain way as a reaction to your typical ball flight. For example, if you slice, you may start aligning to the left to make room for your left-to-right curve. The opposite goes for the golfer who tends to hook. But these are individual variations we cannot cover here, so let's establish a method for setting a square clubface and square alignment. You can vary from the model as necessary.

Starting from behind the ball, pick an intermediate target—an old divot hole, a patch of discolored grass—a few feet in front of the ball and directly on your target line. Walk to the side of the ball and set the clubhead behind it, positioning the leading edge (bottom) of the clubface perpendicular to your target line. This is where that intermediate target becomes helpful. It's much easier to square your clubface to a spot a few feet away than to a target a couple of hundred yards away.

Using the square clubface as a guide, position your feet, setting your stance line perpendicular to

First, square your clubface to your intermediate target.

Then, align your body parallel to the target line.

the clubface, which is also parallel to the target line. Check to see that imaginary lines across your knees, hips, and shoulders are all parallel to your stance. If they are, you have a square clubface and square alignment to match.

BEST TIP: Use an Aiming Station

Proper aim and alignment come from good habits. You have to learn to establish your target line and use it to aim your club and align your body.

To d o this, set up an aiming station the next time you go to the practice range. Lay down a 12- to 15-foot piece of rope to represent the line you want the shot to start on, then place a club on the ground in front of your toes and parallel to the rope. Lining up your feet with this club will effectively square your stance.

Hit some balls from this setup, first setting the leading edge of the clubface perpendicular to the rope, then setting your body lines parallel to the club on the ground. Getting into the habit of squaring the clubface and then matching your body will serve you well on the course.

—Jim Flick, *GOLF Magazine*
Master Teaching Professional

Ball Position and Stance

Of all the preswing elements, stance and ball position are probably the most instinctual. Ball position relies heavily on innate eye–hand coordination. Plus, you get direct feedback: If you're hitting behind the ball, it's too far forward; if you're hitting the top of it, it's too far back. Even rank beginners figure that out. And your stance is simply a way of arranging your feet to maintain balance during the swing, which you do naturally to support any motion.

The downside to these elements becoming second nature so quickly is that golfers tend to forget about them. As they gain more knowledge of the mechanics of the swing, they have "bigger fish to fry" than these elementary setup positions. Such thinking is a grave error, for although ball position and stance may not be exciting, they have a tremendous impact on performance. And they, too, can slip off track.

Take ball position. It's one of the first things Tour pros check when their ball-striking starts to slide. If this surprises you, consider why it's important in the first place. In order to fully benefit from the power and precision you work to create in your golf swing, you must hit the ball flush. To do this, you have to make contact with the ball at precisely the right point during the swing—or else your effort is wasted.

So where is this right point? With the driver, it's just after the clubhead has passed the low point in its arc and started to ascend. For all other shots, contact should come just before the clubhead reaches the low point. Remember, nothing ensures solid contact better than proper ball position.

Where to Play the Ball

Although many great players, including Jack Nicklaus, have been successful playing the ball in the same position for all shots, it's generally accepted

Play the driver off the left heel for a square hit.

Center the ball for the wedge for a descending blow.

today that the ball should move progressively farther back in the stance as the clubs get shorter.

First, understand that the swing will tend to bottom out directly below the swing center, or the
sternum. The key to solid ball-striking is having

the ball positioned so that you create the right sternum-to-ball relationship at impact—sternum behind the ball for the driver, about over the ball for a 5-iron, and slightly in front of the ball for a wedge.

If the driver is played off the left heel, as most teachers recommend, the 5-iron should be two to three inches behind that, and the wedge in about the middle of the stance. Why such big changes? With the longer clubs, the golfer moves aggressively toward the target on the downswing, which moves the swing arc forward and requires a forward ball position. With the shorter clubs, there's little lateral body thrust toward the target and therefore the ball should be played below the sternum to create the proper impact.

Customize Your Ball Position

You can easily determine your optimum ball position with each club based on your own individual swing. Grab your driver, 5-iron, and pitching wedge and find any flat grassy area. Starting with the wedge, make some normal practice swings, noting where the clubhead cuts through the grass. Do the same with your 5-iron, then your driver, marking their respective touchdown points with tees.

The location of the tees will tell you where you should position the ball for each club. Keep in mind, the exact ball position should be slightly behind the touchdown points for the irons, as you want to make ball-first contact. For the driver, position the ball slightly in front of the touchdown spot to promote a slight upswing hit. With a little experimentation, you'll identify the optimum ball position for the various clubs; then it's just a matter of keeping tabs on it from shot to shot and round to round.

BEST TIP: Distance from the Ball

Golfers often ask me how far they should stand from the ball. To answer them, I refer to a composite computer model that Dr. Ralph Mann and I generated from a biomechanical study using 54 PGA Tour pros. With the driver, the pros we tested addressed the ball with their left toe approximately 32 inches from the ball. Shorter golfers may want to increase that to 33 inches, taller players to 31. For a 5-iron, the pros stood 23 to 25 inches away; with a 9-iron, 19 to 21 inches. So, the next time you go to practice, slip a yardstick in your bag and see how you measure up.

—Fred Griffin, *GOLF Magazine* Top 100 Teacher

Good Standing

We've touched on the stance already, but let's take a more in-depth look at the basic rules. There are really two areas to consider when you position your feet: how wide apart to set them and how to angle them in relation to the target line. Your stance should never be wider than it has to be for stability, as a wide stance restricts the natural motion of the hips and legs. In general, as the clubs become shorter, your stance should become narrower, your narrowest stance coming with the wedges. This is because the shorter clubs produce a steeper swinging motion and limited weight transfer and therefore don't require a wide stance for balance. The faster, more powerful swings made with the longer clubs produce weight transfer and rely on a wider stance for stability.

So how wide is right? Picture vertical lines drawn down from your shoulders. With a wedge, the outer edges of your feet should line up with these vertical lines; with a 5-iron, the middle of your feet should be on the lines; and with the driver, your insteps should correspond with the lines. Flexible players can spread their feet a bit more, but keep in mind, the more you widen your stance, the more you restrict body coil.

With a wedge, set the outsides of your feet at shoulder width.

Angling the feet at address also has a major influence on how the body works during the swing. Assuming the stance is square to the target, flaring either foot outward affects the body's turning capacity. If you flare out the right foot, the hips and therefore the shoulders turn more easily away from the target. Turn out the left foot and you facilitate

With a driver, set your insteps at shoulder width.

body turn toward the target on the downswing. Try these variations; you'll feel the difference.

Many teachers recommend a square right foot, set at a right angle to the target line, and a slightly flared left foot, opened roughly 20 degrees toward the target. Squaring the right foot limits the hip turn going back, providing resistance as the torso

A square right foot creates a tight backswing coil.

turns and letting the body coil like a spring. Flaring the left foot presets a quick uncoiling of the lower body on the downswing, a powerful move all golfers should strive for.

BEST TIP: A Guide for Wide

Your stance should never be wider than your normal walking stride. Most golfers err on the wide side, as they feel more powerful. Ironically, a wide stance actually reduces power by restricting body turn.

Here's how to establish your ideal stance width: Take a normal step forward with your left foot and stop. Spin 90 degrees to your right, keeping your toes in place. That's how wide you should stand with the driver. For each successive club, narrow your stance a half inch, which puts your feet five to six inches closer together for the short irons.

—John Redman, *GOLF Magazine*
Top 100 Teacher

Posture

Good posture, whether it be at the dinner table or walking down the street, makes a person look alert and confident. Poor posture, on the other hand, suggests sloppiness and fatigue and makes a person seem careless and decidedly less athletic.

In life, such generalizations may be unfair, but when it comes to golf, they do hold some truth. Fact is, the better your posture at address, the better your chance of making a powerful, consistent golf swing. This is not to suggest that your back has to be ramrod-straight, with your chin jutting high in the air; rather you should find a balance between textbook-perfect posture and posture that is comfortable for you.

Physics and kinesiology tell us there are ideal angles at which the body moves fastest and most efficiently. But when a golfer cannot easily create these angles at address or sustain them during the swing, he must make adjustments to his setup or else risk in-swing compensations. For example, a person with rounded shoulders should naturally slump over more than a person who has perfect posture. Point is, strained positions create tension, and tension is the number-one killer of golf swings.

It's a Balancing Act

One of the irksome things about this game is that the golf ball lies on the ground and the golfer stands almost upright. Immediately you're faced with a dilemma: how to get the clubhead down to the ball. There are two primary ways to lower yourself toward the ball: Tilt the torso forward (upper body) and flex the knees (lower body). Sounds easy enough, until you learn that effective posture is a delicate balance of the two.

For starters, the upper body should pitch forward from the hip sockets while the knees assume a

To set your posture, first tilt forward from the hips.

slight or "athletic" flex, like those of a tennis player awaiting a serve. The order in which you introduce these angles is critical: You must tilt the upper body first, which sets your weight forward, then you flex your knees just enough to redistribute the weight toward the middle of the feet. If you start with the knees, you'll tend to bend them too much and then

After you've pitched forward, add a slight flex to the knees.

set the upper body too upright, the most common posture fault among amateurs.

Once you assume your posture, you should feel balanced and stable, as if you could react in any direction without losing your footing. Golf is unlike many other sports in that you're not physically reacting to an opponent's moves; but in the case of

address posture, try nevertheless to create a
"ready" or "anticipatory" position, as if some action
were coming your way.

BEST TIP: Get Vertically Aligned

The body posture to strive for at address is
called "vertical alignment." This is a fancy way
of saying you want your upper body balanced
over your lower body. More specifically, you
achieve this position if a straight line extending
downward from the back of your shoulders
(viewed from the side) would pass through
your kneecaps and into the balls of your feet.
Have a friend hang a club from the back of
either shoulder to see how you line up at
address.

—Rick McCord, *GOLF Magazine*
Top 100 Teacher

A Second Tilt

Besides tilting toward the ball, your upper body
should also tilt a few degrees away from the target
at address. This slight lean to the right presets the
coiling action of the upper body and weight trans-

Good Advice Gone Bad

Beginning golfers are constantly being told to keep their head down, because they tend to look up prematurely to see the shot. As a result of these constant reminders, many golfers become "ball bound," meaning they fixate on the ball at address. When this happens, the head invariably droops down, burying the chin in the chest. Then, when the shoulders try to turn on the backswing, the chin gets in the way and thereby cuts off the coiling action and shortens the swing. To prevent this, remind yourself at address to keep your head up and look at the ball through the bottoms of your eyes.

fer to the right leg on the backswing. The good news is, this tilt occurs naturally—if you let it.

Here's what happens: When a right-handed golfer grips a club, he places his right hand below his left on the handle, by about four inches. This position drops the right shoulder lower than the left and, since the shoulders are connected to the spine, tilts the spine slightly to the right. From there, the body will "load" onto the right side as the backswing is completed, setting up a powerful return to the ball.

There's more. When your spine tilts to the right, your head has little choice but to go with it. And that's a beneficial position as well, as your head needs to be behind the ball through impact to maximize the power and leverage of the swing.

Placing your right hand below your left on the grip tilts your spine away from the target.

Preshot Routine

Now that we've discussed the preswing components, we need to consider a system for putting
them into place before every swing. This may

Is Your "K" Okay?

One of the most enduring images in golf instruction is the reverse "K" address position. It's created by the slight tilting of the spine away from the target. To see it, take your address facing a full-length mirror.

Draw an imaginary line from your left foot to your left shoulder; it should be fairly straight and tilt slightly away from the target. Then envision a similar line along your right side. It should run from your right shoulder to your waist, then kink and go down your right leg. Together these two lines should resemble the letter "K" turned backward. Check this position often, as it promotes many correct moves in the golf swing.

sound like a lot to keep track of, but the good news is human beings are creatures of habit: We thrive on the familiarity that habit brings. The trick is to make sure you form the right habits, which then serve as a barrier to keep the wrong ones out.

What you need is a sensible method for organizing the various elements of the setup. The best way to do this is to establish a preshot routine, a series of simple preparation tasks designed to get you physically and mentally ready to execute the shot at hand. As you think about making a preshot routine part of your game, remember that the better your setup, the better your odds of consistently making an effective golf swing. Address positions are literally the foundation of the swing. Get them right and you have something reliable on which to build.

Why All the Fuss?

The purpose of the preshot routine is twofold. First, it provides a logical framework for organizing the setup components; and second, it creates a consistent approach from one shot to the next. A good preshot routine ensures that you give due diligence to the setup and then sends you into the swing feeling confident and relaxed, knowing you've done everything possible to prepare yourself. This way you can ask your body to execute a golf swing and reasonably expect it to respond.

For starters, understand that in the moments preceding every shot, your mind and body will be engaged in some form of activity. If you use that time well, meaning you establish your setup and promote relaxation, you're putting yourself in position to perform well. If you use that time unwisely, thinking about too many things or just fidgeting over the ball, your performance is a crapshoot. The first step to consistent performance is consistent preparation.

Next time you watch the pros on television, notice how they all perform their own preshot routine. Some look simple; others seem elaborate and tedious. But the common denominator is they repeat their routine before every shot they play. They know that golf is a complicated game, and the more you can standardize it from shot to shot, the more you simplify it. So stop reinventing the wheel every time you step up to your ball. Start with an effective preshot routine and your performance and confidence level will soar.

A Few Preshot Guidelines

It's true that every preshot routine has its own personality, but that's not to say they don't have common components. Every routine should start with an assessment of the target area and should end with a relaxation check just before the start of the swing. In between, the various setup elements should be established, and extraneous thoughts and actions should be kept to an absolute minimum.

The best starting place for any shot is directly behind the ball, where you can clearly view the target area and envision the ball flight in your mind. This signals the start of your preshot routine, indicating it's time to clear your mind of any negative thoughts and to focus on creating a perfect setup. The theme from start to finish should be simplicity and structure. In the end, your routine should not be mentally taxing and should be easy to repeat time and time again.

Get a Good View

Standing a few paces behind the ball, first establish your ultimate target. This may not be the middle of the fairway or the flag, due to the proximity of hazards or the ideal angle for your next shot. For instance, if you're a short hitter playing a hole that doglegs to the left 250 yards out, you may want to play to the right side off the tee to set up a clear approach. Whatever the case, pick a target that's realistic for you, always considering your next play.

Keep in mind, your target line probably isn't the line you want to start your shot on. If you tend to curve the ball either left or right, you need to borrow some room to allow for that curve—perhaps 10 to 20 yards. Once you establish a starting line for the shot, pick an intermediate target, as described earlier, directly on that line and a few feet in front of your ball. You'll use this intermediate spot at address to establish precise aim and alignment.

Some players like to take their grip while standing behind the ball, which is fine. Since we've already discussed how to arrange your hands, just note that you must make sure the clubface is square once your grip is complete. To do this, raise the clubhead up to waist level after you've taken your grip: The clubface is square if the leading edge,

From behind the ball, pick an intermediate target directly on your starting line.

or bottom, of the face is perpendicular to the ground. Now you're ready to step into the shot.

Step to the Side

If you wish to take a practice swing, do so as soon as you walk to the side of the ball. Practice swings can be useful in relieving tension or rehearsing a particular swing, but eliminate them if you feel they interrupt the flow of the preshot routine or offer little preparation value. Players who lack patience or find themselves rushing through the preshot process should consider skipping the practice swing and focusing on the essential preshot elements, such as aim and alignment. It may be reassuring to rehearse your swing, but to do so in lieu of a proper setup is only hurting your chances.

Once you're ready to step up to the ball, your first objective should be to square the clubface to your starting line. Locate your intermediate target, then tilt your upper body forward to lower the clubhead to the ball. Set the leading edge of the clubface behind the ball and perpendicular to your starting line. If you haven't already completed your grip, now's the time to do it—left hand first, then

Square your clubface before taking your stance.

right. Make sure the clubface is square to your starting line when your grip is complete.

Using the clubface as a guide, set your feet parallel to your intended starting line. To do this, it might help to picture your setup as a T square, with your clubface flush to the ruler's edge and the tips of your shoes up against either end of the "T." Although your other body lines tend to follow the alignment of your feet, it's a good idea to run your eyes from your toes to your shoulders, making sure these lines are parallel to one another.

At this point, your body weight should be favoring your toes, as you've tilted your upper body forward to sole the clubhead. To counter this, flex your knees slightly to redistribute the weight toward the middle of each foot. Remember, keep your knee bend to a minimum. Your lower body should feel ready to support the momentum of the swing but not be in a strained or aggressive pose.

One last thing before you start your swing: Check your relaxation level. Tension at address leads to a fast takeaway and limited range of motion. The two most popular ways to curb tension are waggling the clubhead and taking deep breaths. The waggle keeps your hands and arms supple so they can create a smooth start to the swing, while deep breathing can relieve muscle tension throughout your body. Although it's a good idea to monitor your breathing throughout the preshot process, the most important time is just before you start the club back. Feel the breathing down in your diaphragm, not just in your upper chest. The relaxation you create will really pay off.

It's a Golfer's Best Friend

Golf at times seems a cruel and lonely game. But with an effective preshot routine on your side, you can create a sense of familiarity and reassurance be-

---

A Sample Preshot Routine

Behind the ball:

1. Pick your target and starting line for the shot.
2. Select an intermediate target in front of the ball.
3. Complete your grip.

Beside the ball:

4. Make a practice swing to rehearse the feel.
5. Using the intermediate target, square the clubface.
6. Using the square clubface, align your body.
7. Complete your posture.
8. Relaxation check: waggle or deep breath.

---

fore every swing you make. It's a lot easier to be relaxed over the ball knowing you've achieved the correct setup positions and done all you can to ready your mind and body.

Furthermore, a reliable preshot routine will do wonders for your performance under pressure. When a stressful situation arises, such as teeing off in front of a crowd or playing sudden death in a match, most golfers either speed up or try to carefully control every step of the process. The speedsters wind up swinging before they've adequately prepared their mind or body, while the deliberate types only add to the gravity of the moment. The key in pressure situations is using the same routine you've grooved when the pressure wasn't on; that's the best way to counter the anxiety you feel.

BEST TIP: Perform at Peak Concentration

The amount of time it takes to perform the preshot routine is critical yet often overlooked. Each golfer has his own capacity to concentrate, and for every shot he faces, there's one moment in time when his concentration is at its peak. Your objective should be to reach that peak and act then.

Over the years, I've timed about 50 PGA Tour players to see how long they take to hit a shot. Three-quarters of them took between 18 and 22 seconds from the moment they clicked "on" their concentration to contact with the ball. Each had his own preshot routine, which never varied from shot to shot, and each took a consistent amount of time to hit the ball.

Experiment with preshot routines of varying lengths on the practice range and have a friend time each one with a stopwatch. Over time, your performance and patience level will tell you if you need a concise or detailed approach. Once you know, create a preshot routine to fit your concentration capacity and then use it before every swing you make.

—Dr. Richard Coop, *GOLF Magazine*
Mental Game Consultant

The Swing

Think of the golf swing like a game of dominoes: Set it up, get it started, and the rest takes care of itself. Okay, it's not quite that simple, but the swing *is* a natural chain of events—and doesn't have to be as complicated as many amateurs make it. With all the mental and physical factors you can try to control, it's no wonder the average player often seems frustrated and confused. He is, much of the time, simply overwhelmed.

But it doesn't have to be that way. First of all, understand that the outcome of your shots is largely determined by decisions you make before you step up to the ball, such as club selection, shot selection, and target orientation. If any of these factors are off, your outcome will suffer despite how well you execute your swing. It's during the preswing period that the golfer has to be a thinker.

After these preliminary decisions, your focus becomes the setup, which we've established as a major factor in performance. How major? Look at it this way: You take your setup—a structured, step-by-step procedure—and all that's left is making the swing itself, which should be an instinctive, flowing action. This is where athleticism must take over.

Remember, almost all of the thinking you do on a given shot should be completed before you take the club back. The angles and positions we are about to discuss should be grooved on the practice tee, not on the golf course. Mechanical thoughts cause tension, and tension is your swing's biggest enemy. So, consider yourself forewarned: Think while you practice and before you execute. Once you start your swing, rely as much as possible on your athletic instincts.

Starting Back

Put simply, the takeaway sets the shape and pace of the golf swing. A swing that starts off smoothly, the arms and body moving in sync, has a good chance of producing favorable results. One that starts quickly or out of sequence demands in-swing compensations, which are unreliable at best.

There are several keys to a good takeaway. First of all, it should not start from a still position, one good reason to waggle the club at address, as described earlier. Another effective preswing motion is the forward press, whereby the golfer pushes his hands slightly toward the target immediately before starting the club back. In this case, the takeaway is essentially a rebound of the forward press.

Starting back, the hands, arms, and shoulders should move the club away together. This is called a "one-piece takeaway." Such connection at the start is critical to creating the right path and shape for the swing. You should feel like the left shoulder is pushing the club back, without any conscious twisting or hinging of the hands or wrists.

When the clubhead reaches hip high, there are three important positions to check. First, the shaft should be parallel to the target line, the butt end of the grip pointing just left of the target. Second, there should only be a slight hinge in the

Tailor Your Waggle

Aside from kick-starting the swing, the waggle can also serve as a rehearsal of your takeaway. Consider this: Most golfers either lift the club abruptly on the takeaway or else drag it back with tense arms and stiff wrists. If you have either problem, design a waggle to prevent it. Use a wide, one-piece waggle to head off an abrupt start, or a loose, wristy waggle to avoid a rigid, mechanical takeaway. Take advantage of your rehearsal.

2ls __
ls __
le __

At hip high, the shaft should be parallel to the target line.

During the takeaway, the wrists should hinge only slightly.

left wrist, as this initial move is a wide, sweeping motion. And third, the toe of the clubhead should be turned upward, as the forearms naturally start to rotate. With the clubhead hip high, the leading edge of the clubface should match the forward tilt of your spine. Get these positions right and you've created a wide extension and the proper path for your golf swing.

The only other factor to consider on the takeaway is tempo. This needs to be the slowest part of your swing. If the takeaway is fast or abrupt, the swing will follow suit; likewise, if you start with a smooth, wide extension, you're likely to maintain good rhythm and width throughout your swing. So remember, think slow at the start: The swing is plenty long enough to produce acceleration without any quick bursts of speed in the early going.

BEST TIP: Get a Head Start

To groove a wide, smooth extension away from the ball, hit some practice shots starting from a fully extended postimpact position. (Set up as usual, then move the clubhead out a few feet toward the target, fully extending your arms as you do after impact.) From there, just take your normal backswing. Starting from a full extension (see photo at right) promotes a wide, smooth move going back.

—Dick Tiddy, *GOLF Magazine* Top 100 Teacher

To the Top

Once the clubhead reaches hip high, the majority of the body weight should already be on the right instep. This weight transfer occurs as a natural result of the arms and shoulders extending the clubhead away from the ball. If your weight is still centered at this point, chances are you've made an

BEST TIP: Try the exercise described on the previous page to groove a good takeaway.

abrupt takeaway by lifting the club with your hands and cocking your wrists.

From the hip-high position, the wrists will start to hinge the club upward, as long as they are free of excess tension. In fact, by the time the hands are opposite the right ear, the wrists should have cocked the club into a 90-degree angle with the left arm, creating a distinct second lever in the swing. This second lever not only allows the clubhead to swing through a much longer arc in the backswing, but also sets up a powerful release of energy on the downswing. Wrist cock is one of the hallmarks of a powerful swing.

Just Plane Talk

Swing plane is a daunting topic to many golfers, so let's simplify it. The plane of the golf swing is established by the angle of the shaft to the ground at address (looking down the target line). As a general rule, a swing is called "on plane" if the club stays parallel to this address angle throughout the swing. Longer clubs create a flatter plane, as the golfer stands farther from the ball to accommodate the longer shafts, while shorter clubs put the golfer closer to the ball and therefore produce a more upright swing plane. But while the shaft angle at ad-

Going back, the wrists should hinge the club into a 90-degree angle with the left arm.

dress varies from club to club, the shaft should stay roughly parallel to this starting angle throughout the swing—and that goes for every club in the bag.

To further understand the concept of swinging on plane, picture your target line extending infinitely both toward and away from the target. At address, the shaft points directly at this line. As the club starts back, it sweeps inside and starts to elevate, but the shaft still points directly at the extended target line. As the swing progresses and the wrists hinge, the club turns upside down. Now the butt end of the club points to the extended target line. In fact, either the clubhead end or the butt end, whichever is closer to the ground, should point to this extended line throughout the entire swing.

Although the plane of the swing actually should get slightly flatter coming down than it was going back—as the forward thrust of the lower body on the downswing pulls the club into a flatter position—for simplicity's sake, stick to the extended target line image to check your swing plane.

Load Before You Fire

The purpose of the backswing is to position the club and coil the body in such a way that the downswing

At halfway back, the grip end should point to the ball.

is a simple reversal of events. As I've said, the farther along you get, the harder it is to assert control over the swing; by the time the downswing begins, if not sooner, you have to be on automatic pilot.

After the wrists have fully hinged, the hips and shoulders continue to turn to complete the backswing. It's important to remember that once the shoulders stop turning, the arms should stop swinging back. If they don't, the body will likely start down before the arms are ready, throwing the swing out of sync. Ideally, the shoulders turn 90 degrees and the hips 45 degrees from their starting positions to the top of the backswing. This relationship between the upper body and lower body coils the torso like a spring, setting up a powerful uncoiling on the downswing.

Now let's discuss the role of the lower body in the backswing. Most teachers view the lower body as the support base for the actions of the upper body. As such, the legs do not initiate any backswing action. In fact, the lower body should resist the turning of the upper body to create the springlike effect that will power the downswing. In short, the legs should simply maintain their flex and react to the coiling of the torso, the right leg serving as the axis over which the upper body rotates.

If the lower body stays passive, the torso coils like a spring.

BEST TIP: *Light Up Your Line*

Here's a good visual for checking your swing plane. Line up two clubs on the ground, one on either side of the ball, to represent your target line. Then tape two flashlights together end to end, so the beams shine in opposite directions. Grip the flashlights like a club and take your setup, shining one beam on the ball. Take some slow-motion half-swings: If your swing is perfectly on-plane, the beam from one flashlight, then the other should shine on the clubs going back. Coming down, again one beam, then the other should track along the clubs.

—Rick Grayson, *GOLF Magazine*
Top 100 Teacher

Checkpoints at the Top

The top of the backswing offers one last chance to check yourself before "letting it go." Not that you should have swing thoughts at this point; your thinking should be geared toward the setup and maybe the very early part of the swing. But, when practicing, it is useful to swing to the top and assess what your swing looks and feels like. The downswing happens too fast to include reliable compensations for bad positions at the top.

At the top, the upper body should feel fully coiled, with the left shoulder turned under the chin. The left arm should be fairly straight, although not stiff, and the back of the left hand should be in a straight line with the left forearm, neither cupped nor bowed. Ideally, the club should be parallel to your target line and in a fully horizontal position. A square clubface at the top, assuming you've swung it all the way back, puts the leading edge at the same angle as your left forearm—roughly 45 degrees to the ground.

The lower body should feel stable and ready to start moving toward the target. Most of the body weight should be distributed between the right instep and heel, never to the outside of the right foot, and the left knee should be kicked in slightly.

Most golfers keep their left heel planted throughout the backswing, although inflexible players may consider letting the momentum of the backswing pull it an inch or two off the ground to allow for a fuller swing. Nevertheless, even if the heel is lifted, the left toe should still be gripping the ground, as the body must be in position to shift left and drive toward the target.

For a full coil, feel your left shoulder turn under your chin.

Stay in Those Angles

An effective backswing winds the body up and sets the club in a position at the top from which it is easy to simply reverse directions and deliver the club forcefully to the ball. The key word here is "simply," as many golfers make moves on the backswing that have to be undone on the down-swing if the clubhead is to accurately return to the ball.

The most important area when it comes to keeping your swing simple is posture. In short, you have to maintain the same body posture from address through impact in order to achieve any degree of ball-striking consistency. If your posture changes going back, meaning you raise up or shrink down, you have to make the exact reversal of that move on the downswing to strike the ball solidly.

As noted earlier, posture is a combination of forward tilt from the hips and flex in the knees. Although these critical body angles vary from player to player, based on individual physique, once they're established at address, they must remain fixed through contact with the ball. This can be a challenging endeavor, especially for less flexible players, since the address position can feel awkward even before the body starts coiling.

To add to the difficulty, the coiling action of the backswing jeopardizes these angles in two ways. First, it's easier to turn your shoulders from a more upright position, which encourages you to raise up as the shoulders near their rotational limit. Second, as weight transfers to your back foot, it's easy to let it drift to the outside of the foot, which often causes

> ## BEST TIP: Feel a Good Coil
>
> Coil is created when you wind the upper body against the resistance of the lower body. To feel this, sit on a bench or chair and lean forward 30 degrees. Grip a club and start to swing back, turning your left shoulder toward your chin. Since you can't turn your hips at all while sitting, you'll feel the large muscles of your back start to stretch almost immediately. Try to reproduce this coiled feeling in your golf swing.
>
> —Carl Lohren, *GOLF Magazine* Top 100 Teacher

the back knee to straighten. These tendencies make it all the more important to be aware of maintaining your posture through impact.

One good way to make sure you're staying in posture is to swing in front of a full-length mirror with a mark or piece of tape indicating your head level at address. Swing back and through several times, looking up to check that your head doesn't move above or below its starting position until it turns up on the follow-through.

The Transition

We've said that the takeaway sets the overall shape and pace of the swing, but the transition from backswing to downswing has the most direct effect on the shape and pace of the down-swing. In other words, the way the golfer changes direction at the top in large part determines his position at impact, which is the only position that dictates where the ball goes.

The keys to a good transition are proper sequence of motion and smooth tempo. Most teachers hold that the downswing should occur from the ground up, starting with a weight transfer or lateral "bump" back to the front foot. From there, the body should start un-winding, lower body leading and pulling the upper body, until the club is pulled through by the momentum of this uncoiling action. There need be no conscious flipping of the hands through the hitting area: If the body is allowed to unwind in sequence, centrifugal force will properly position the hands and arms at impact.

> **Don't Pause**
>
> Players who tend to rush the club back down to the ball are often told to pause at the top. This is danger-ous advice for two reasons. First, the swing should al-ways be thought of as one flowing motion: Any con-scious starting or stopping disrupts its natural rhythm. Second, a pause at the top reduces the resistance be-tween the upper and lower body, promoting a down-swing in which the entire body unwinds together. The result is a lack of lever-age on the downswing and a dramatic loss of power.

If the downswing is simply a reversal of the back-swing, it must begin with a return of the weight to the front foot. In fact, the lower body actually should

The downswing starts with a lateral "bump" back to the front foot.

start toward the target a split second before the upper body finishes turning back. This stretches the muscles involved in the coil even more and gives the appearance that the clubhead lags behind in the downswing sequence. The immortal Bobby Jones described this action in his book *Golf Is My Game* as follows, "The all-important feel which I experience as the swing changes direction is one of leaving the clubhead at the top of the swing."

BEST TIP: *Uncoil from the Ground Up*

Grip a three-foot-long piece of rope as if it were a golf club and swing it back, letting it flip over your right shoulder. From there, swing the rope down and through, letting the lower body lead the uncoiling action, pulling the rope taut and making the tip trail through the hitting area. This drill proves that the downswing is a pulling motion, as the lower body must lead the upper body for the tip of the rope to whip through last.

—Martin Hall, *GOLF Magazine*
Master Teaching Professional

Watch Your Speed

Just like the first move away from the ball, the transition from backswing to downswing should be smooth and unhurried. In fact, a graceful transition is one of the most aesthetically pleasing parts of the golf swing.

Think of the great players you like to watch. I'll bet they include such smooth swingers as Fred Couples, Ernie Els, and Steve Elkington. These players seem to have effortless power—no sudden bursts of speed, yet an aggressive whip into the ball. Much of this graceful power comes from a smooth transition, which allows them to gradually accelerate the club through impact. The simple truth is that the more you rush the swing from the top, the less speed you'll have at impact. Your swing can only have one fast point—save it for when it counts.

If you think smooth tempo is an intangible quality and either you have it or you don't, you're half right. The world's top golfers are gifted athletes with a natural sense of rhythm and timing, but that doesn't mean you can't improve your own speed control. If you can calm the instinct to "hit from the top" and trust that gradual acceleration will yield maximum swing speed, you'll groove a more powerful, more consistent golf swing.

How to Find "The Slot"

If, as we've said, an effective downswing should simply undo the positions achieved on the backswing, this means the arms, which travel in and up going back, must reverse that motion so that they move down and out—in that order. Unfortunately, most golfers don't let the club drop down before they swing it out to the ball. As we'll see later, the "over-the-top" downswing that results is one of the most prevalent faults in the game.

The fall of the arms at the start of the downswing is one of the marks of an accomplished player. The good news is, it's a move that happens naturally if you follow the correct sequence of motion from the top. In other words, you don't have to consciously pull your arms down; a proper transition will drop them into position.

Let me explain. From a fully wound position at the top, your first move down—a lateral shift back to your front foot—will cause your arms to drop downward toward your right side. As the uncoiling of the body begins, the left shoulder pulls away from the chin, which also pulls the arms downward. Again, this dropping action is merely a response to the body's move toward the target, not a conscious action.

If the arms remain passive at the start of the downswing, they will fall into a position called "the slot," with the right elbow tucked close to the right side, the wrists still fully hinged, and the butt of the club pointing to the ball. This position sets the stage for a powerful delivery from inside the target line. Virtually all good ballstrikers, despite any idiosyncrasies on the backswing,

Don't Get Down

The idea that you have to hit down on the ball is one of the biggest misconceptions in the game. Truth is, the club should move at about a 90-degree angle to the spine on the downswing. The up-and-down appearance of the swing is created by the forward tilt of the spine at address. The golf swing is very much like a baseball swing; it just starts from a more bent-over position.

If the arms stay passive at the start of the downswing, the club drops into "the slot."

drop the club into the slot. Stay relaxed and let your swing unwind and you can, too.

Through Impact

Once you get into the downswing, you've reached the point of no return. You simply cannot manipulate the swing from this point forward with any degree of consistency. You've had your chances to affect the fate of the shot at hand, from club selection to setup positions to even a simple thought at the change of direction. Now the swing is on its own. The flight of the ball will tell you how well you've done.

This is not to suggest that you shouldn't be sensing anything through impact, only that trying to time specific positions when the club should be freewheeling into the ball is unwise and unreliable. You can, and should, feel certain sensations as the body uncoils, but they are "flowing" sensations that occur throughout the downswing. Among them are the transition of weight to the front foot and the pulling of the torso and arms by the lower body. Let's try to isolate these feelings and thereby create a sensory framework for the downswing. You may not be able to "save the swing" at this point, but you can sense how it's going.

Shift, Then Turn

While the lower body plays only a supporting role on the backswing, it takes center stage at the change of direction. After the initial forward shift of the lower body, the hips should start to rotate aggressively toward the target. This rotation, or "clearing," of the hips gives the downswing its rotary shape

After the weight shifts forward, the hips start rotating to the target.

and also preserves the resistance between the upper and lower halves created on the backswing. Maintaining this resistance well into the downswing allows you to unleash the power of the coil at impact.

By now the majority of the weight should be on the front foot. It's worth noting again that sequence

BEST TIP: *Attack from the Inside*

To groove an inside path into impact, practice hitting balls with your right foot pulled back 12 inches from its normal position and set on its toe. Make a normal swing from this stance and your right arm and shoulder will naturally drop to the inside as the swing changes direction, setting up a powerful in-to-out path through impact. Hit several balls from this stance and then try to incorporate the feeling into your normal swing.

—Jane Frost, *GOLF Magazine* Top 100 Teacher

of motion is crucial: Your lower body must lead the way, first with a lateral weight shift to the front foot, then with a rapid rotation of the hips. Since the hips turn fairly level, the unwinding force they create drops the club onto a flatter, more rotary plane, which brings the clubhead downward. This flattening of the swing plane sets up a powerful approach from the inside.

With the weight shifting forward, the left leg will serve as the axis around which the upper body turns through the ball, just as the right leg functioned on the backswing. This aggressive shifting and turning of the lower body clears a path for the hands and arms to deliver the club from the slot position—the key to strong, accurate ball-striking.

Narrowing of the Arc

A powerful swing features a distinct narrowing of the clubhead arc on the downswing. To understand this, consider a simple image. If the clubhead left a trail in the air like a skywriting plane, the downswing part of the trail, viewed from a face-to-face position with the golfer, would be much narrower, or closer to the body, than the backswing portion. It would look as if the golfer has yanked the grip in closer to his body on the downswing. This narrowing of the arc proves that the proper sequence of motion has occurred and also indicates stored power.

When the lower body leads the downswing, the right shoulder and arm are pulled downward, dropping the right elbow to the right side. Compare this position to its backswing counterpart and you'll notice there were several inches between the right elbow and the body going back, giving the backswing its wide, sweeping shape. By contrast, the right elbow virtually rides on the body coming down. Furthermore, the wrists are still fully cocked when the hands reach hip high in the downswing, which is exactly where the wrists *started* to cock on the backswing. This sharp wrist angle dramatically shortens the return path of the clubhead.

There is another reason the clubhead arc appears so much narrower on the downswing: the lateral shift of the hips. On aggressive full swings, the hips move about six inches toward the target at the start of the downswing—the "bump" I referred to earlier. This lateral move shifts the clubhead arc six inches forward. So, while the clubhead actually does stay closer to the body on the downswing, the repositioning of the lower body serves to exaggerate this narrowing effect.

> ### BEST TIP: Check Your Width
> To make sure you have the right sequence of motion on your downswing, compare your clubhead arc halfway down to its position halfway back. Set up next to a bush or small tree so that your clubhead just reaches the leaves halfway back. Then take some practice swings, stopping to check the clubhead position halfway down. Your lateral move toward the target to start the downswing and the subsequent body rotation should pull the clubhead at least a foot inside the leaves on the downswing.
>
> —Craig Shankland, *GOLF Magazine* Top 100 Teacher

Your Power Source

It's easy to say that brute force has no place in the golf swing. It's decidedly more difficult to sell this idea to a golfer who has just seen Tiger Woods or John Daly hit a tee shot. The explosion of power that these great players produce at impact makes it seem that they are attacking the ball with every ounce of energy they have.

Although they may be doing just that, it is important to remember that they are employing swinging force, not hitting force. That's the difference: The pros let the clubhead swing through the ball, while average golfers throw the club at the ball. Impact is not a position to the pros; it is simply an action that occurs between the backswing and the follow-through. To borrow an age-old saying, "The ball just gets in the way."

That's not to say that strength is not a power factor in golf. But upper-body strength typically associated with muscular people—the upper arms, chest, and shoulders—actually does little for the golf swing. The strength and flexibility of the trunk and the core muscles (abdomen and lower back) have a much greater impact on your power potential than a muscular upper body. We've all seen our share of muscle-bound strongmen who can't hit the ball 200 yards off the tee. You wouldn't tell them they lack power—if you're smart—yet they are not powerful golfers.

So where does the power come from? Most of it is generated by the tension created as the upper body coils around the lower body. The more you can wind the torso against the resistance of the hips and

---

Clubhead Follows Grip

Wherever the grip end of the club points on the downswing is where the clubhead will swing through the hitting area. When the club drops into the slot, the butt end should point at the ball. As the swing continues, the butt should turn upward and point to the right of the target, indicating an on-plane swing and an approach from the inside. If the butt of the club points left of the target, the clubhead will swing out to in through impact, and the ball will tend to start to the left. If you slice, you probably suffer from this over-the-top move.

legs, the more power you will store going back and then unleash coming down. This pivoting action of the body relies more on flexibility than strength: You'd much rather have elastic muscles that can produce the winding and unwinding motion than hulking muscles that limit your range of motion.

Other factors in creating power include weight transfer and your body's lever system. Driving your weight to the target on the downswing is critical because it initiates the uncoiling process and establishes the left side as the point of resistance for the full release of the right side through impact. As with so many aspects of the swing, weight transfer on the downswing is set up by the proper loading on the backswing. In other words, there's no weight to transfer if the backswing didn't do its job—yet another reason to focus on the early part of the swing.

BEST TIP: Towel Drill

Train yourself not to rush the club down from the top by making practice swings with a towel wrapped around the head of your driver. The air resistance of the towel trains you to build speed gradually on the downswing. With the uncoiling of your torso leading the way, the arms do not waste energy with an early hitting action and the clubhead achieves maximum speed through the bottom of the swing.

—Jeff Warne, *GOLF Magazine* Top 100 Teacher

As for your lever system, the biggest power producer is the wrist cock. When the wrists hinge on the backswing and create that 90-degree angle between the club and the left forearm, they store a tremendous amount of potential energy for the downswing. This is where so many golfers cheat themselves of power: They fully cock their wrists going back and then, in an attempt to create power, release this angle too early in the downswing with a hitting or swatting action. To take advantage of the power you've stored, you have to let centrifugal force unhinge the wrists, pull the left arm and the club into a straight line, and sling the clubhead into the ball. You have to simply let that happen.

Centrifugal force pulls the club in line with the left arm at impact.

The Moment of Truth

While it's true that the golf swing is an intricate chain of events, impact between clubhead and ball is the only position that really matters—the only position that the golf ball reacts to. Impact is when you either cash in on a well-timed, well-ordered move or you pay the piper for shortcuts or compensations taken along the way.

This being the case, you may be wondering why we've spent so much time discussing everything that precedes impact. Why not keep it simple and just describe where you need to be at impact? The answer is easy: because you have no conscious control over what the clubhead is doing when it collides with the

---

BEST TIP: *Extend for Power*

Power hitters maximize swing speed by making a full release of the club and a wide follow-through arc, the left wrist remaining flat and the left arm straight well past impact. To sense this extension, make some practice swings with your driver, letting your right hand slip off the grip as the clubhead approaches the hitting area. Without your right hand, your left arm will fully extend to the target and your left wrist will stay flat, as long as your body keeps rotating.

—T. J. Tomasi, *GOLF Magazine* Top 100 Teacher

ball. The swing is happening too quickly to manipulate the club in any reliable fashion. For this reason, the way you perform your downswing, your backswing, even your setup, is how you affect the position and speed of the clubhead as it reaches the ball.

There are, however, a few sensations you should be aware of through the impact area. First, make sure the clubhead is approaching from slightly inside the target line on a semicircle arc. In fact, on practice swings, you should be able to pick up the blurred path of the clubhead, even though it may be moving at speeds upwards of 100 mph at the bottom of the swing arc. Many good things have to happen in the downswing for the clubhead to approach on this path.

Next, you should feel like your right hand and arm are extending to the target. The old image for this is that you're skipping a stone across the surface of a pond with a sidearm motion, elbow leading the hand until the stone is released. To achieve this sensation, your left side must

Don't Return to Address

Forget the old instruction adage that says get into the same position at impact as you were at address. Although the clubhead must return to the ball, your knees and hips should be several inches closer to the target at impact, and your entire torso should be rotated well left. Think of impact as a driving, dynamic move to the target—a brief instant that sometimes eludes even the fastest cameras.

straighten up slightly to provide a point of resistance for the throwing action. Many teachers say you should feel like the right hand and arm make a slapping or spanking motion through the ball.

The important point to remember is that the entire right side should make an aggressive release through impact, aided by centrifugal force and the momen-

Through most of the downswing, the right elbow leads the right hand.

tum of the swing. The long-standing idea that the right side should be passive in the golf swing, so as not to overpower the left, does not apply in the hitting area. In short, no right-handed golfer should suppress the hitting power of his dominant side. Perhaps the legendary Ben Hogan put it best in *Five Lessons: The Modern Fundamentals of Golf* when he said, "As far as applying power goes, I wish that I had three right hands."

To the Finish

With the ball on its way, many golfers think the shot is over and their work is done. Well, you could argue that point, as you can't affect the fate of the ball after it leaves the clubface—despite any midair pleas or threats. You can, however, learn a lot from how you feel after impact and the positions you reach at the finish. Fact is, every motion in the golf swing flows into the follow-through, giving clues as to the correctness of the actions that got you there. Working backward from the finish is one of the most effective learning tools at your disposal.

Let's focus our analysis of the follow-through on three areas: weight transfer, body rotation, and arm swing. First, as you continue to push off the right side and onto the left, your head should remain in its starting position. In fact, it may even move slightly away from the target by impact to counter the driving force of the lower body through the strike. At the finish, all of your weight should be on the outside of your left foot, with your right foot on its toe and serving only to maintain balance.

The body rotation, as it has throughout the downswing, follows the transfer of weight toward the target. The lower body continues to clear the way for the upper body, with the right side now powering the motion and pushing the body into the follow-through. At the finish, the right shoulder should be closer to the target than any other part of the body, and your belt buckle should point slightly left of the target, your chest even farther left. This fully rotated body position proves that the body pulls the arms and the club through impact—the key to maximum leverage and power.

As the body pulls the arms, the right side joins the party and applies some hitting force of its own. The

Heads Up

It's a good idea to let your head swivel in response to the shoulder turn, both on the backswing and downswing. After impact, track your eyes down the target line after the streaking ball, instead of pulling up out of your posture. This will help you maintain your forward tilt through the shot to ensure solid contact. In fact, two of today's top stars, David Duval and Annika Sorenstam, actually rotate their eyes down the line before impact, their heads swiveling, not lifting up.

Relaxed arms naturally rotate and extend through impact.

At the finish, the right shoulder is closest to the target.

right hand and arm fire through the strike, rotating the shaft as the right forearm rolls over the left. This is not a conscious action: If the hands and arms are free of excessive tension through the hitting area, they will naturally release the club. After impact, you should feel like the clubhead is chasing the ball to the target.

The momentum of the swing fully extends the arms toward the target, as the left elbow begins to fold, allowing the club to wrap around the body and run out of steam. One more good flowing sensation: The left elbow should point at the ground throughout the downswing and into the finish. If you can do this, the hands will float up to a position above the left shoulder, as you watch your ball soar to its target.

BEST TIP: *Throw on a Scarf*

To fully release your right hand and arm on the follow-through, imagine you're wrapping a scarf around your neck, throwing it with your right hand. Make some practice swings focusing on this image. It should promote the correct rotation of your right arm and also help keep it relaxed; a stiff right arm restricts your follow-through.

—Mitchell Spearman, *GOLF Magazine*
Top 100 Teacher

Faults

When it comes to swing technique, it's fair to say the end justifies the means. In other words, if you break all the rules of swing mechanics but consistently get the club into a good position at impact, more power to you. No one can argue with good results. As renowned British golf instructor John Jacobs wrote in *The Golf Swing Simplified,* "The golf swing has only one purpose: to deliver the head of the club to the ball correctly. How that is done is immaterial, so long as the method used permits correct impact to be achieved over and over and over again."

That said, you must understand that there are certain parameters when it comes to individual style in the golf swing. Clearly, you can't stray too far from the ideal setup and swing positions discussed in the previous sections and still expect good results on a consistent basis. For example, if you cut across the target line slightly through impact, you may be able to get away with it; but if you slash the club dramatically across the line, impact will be weak and your shots will dart off line. It's all a matter of degree.

But how do you know which faults are acceptable? Your ball flight is your guide. The distance and direction of your shots tells you what happened at impact, which tells you what happened during the swing. It's all very logical. Then you have to decide if you can live with the *good* shots you're hitting. If you can, your focus should be on hitting those good shots more consistently, not overhauling the mechanics of your golf swing. You want to be able to hit serviceable golf shots. Forget about creating textbook swing mechanics. That's something even the best can't emulate.

Look at the great players: They have their own individual swing styles, which often vary greatly. Colin Montgomerie has a long, flowing golf swing, with the hands high on the backswing and again at the finish; David Duval is more around the body, making a powerful trunk rotation back and through. Is one way better than the other? It is for each of these guys. And as good as they are, if one tried to swing like the other, we'd probably never hear from him again.

Point is, there is no perfect golf swing for every-
one. It all boils down to how you position the clubface at impact; that's the acid test of the swing. The
difference between mechanical faults and unorthodox moves is only the results they produce. An un-
conventional swing that consistently delivers good
shots is absolutely flawless. The end truly does jus-
tify the means.

Why Shots Go Where They Go

Before we look at specific faults, it is important to
have a basic understanding of what makes the ball
go where it goes. Simply stated, as the clubhead
swings through impact, the clubface acts on the ball
in several ways. This exchange lasts only half a mil-
lisecond (.0005 of a second) before the ball is on its
way, executing the flight plan by traveling a certain
distance in a certain direction.

This interaction between clubface and ball largely
determines the identity of the shot, along with certain equipment specifications and environmental
conditions. The ball doesn't care if your takeaway is
laughably fast or you lift your head up six inches on
the backswing; it only reacts to the position and
speed of the clubface at impact. This is not to say that
quirky moves cannot have a dramatic effect on the

shot—they do, but only if they influence the clubface at impact. That's why such unorthodox swingers as Lee Trevino, Raymond Floyd, and Jim Furyk have excelled: Their idiosyncrasies allow them—even help them—to deliver the clubface correctly at impact, and that's the only position that really counts.

In all, the clubface "reports to the ball" in five areas. Together, these five impact factors, in large part, produce the outcome of every shot you play. They are in no particular order:

1. Swing path: the path the clubhead takes through the hitting area.

2. Clubface angle: the squareness of the club-face in relation to its path.

3. Clubhead speed: the velocity of the clubhead when it meets the ball.

4. Point of contact: where on the clubface the ball makes contact.

5. Angle of approach: the steepness of the club-head's approach to the ball.

The combined effect of these five impact factors dictates the distance and direction of the ensuing shot. The first two—swing path and clubface angle—largely determine direction, a combination of the

The ball starts in the direction the clubhead takes through the hitting area.

shot's starting direction and any curvature. On full swings, the ball basically starts out in the direction the clubhead takes through the hitting area, as the ball is propelled by forward momentum. If the ball then curves in the air, it means the clubface was not square to this path at the moment of impact.

Distance is a function of the three remaining impact factors. Clubhead speed is the most obvious: The faster the clubhead is moving at impact, the harder the strike and the longer the shot. But club-

The angle of the clubface at impact dictates the way a shot curves.

All else being equal, higher clubhead speed means longer shots.

head speed is wasted if contact is not made on the sweet spot of the clubface; in fact, center-face contact is one of the least discussed yet most important factors in maximizing distance. Off-center hits can also influence shot direction, as they cause a twisting of the clubface through impact, but not as much as swing path or face angle.

> **Face Facts**
>
> On full shots, the path of the clubhead through the hitting area primarily determines the shot's starting direction. In some cases, this is not true, due to a circumstance called "clubface override." In short, this means that if the clubface is dramatically open or closed at impact, it can have more of an influence on starting direction than the path. In effect, the clubface angle overrides the path.

Finally, we have the angle of approach, or how level to the ground the clubhead is traveling when it meets the ball. This incoming angle determines not only the initial launch angle of the shot but also the amount of backspin the clubface imparts on the ball by way of a descending hit. Since backspin creates height and height reduces distance, the approach angle has a major impact on how far the ball goes.

So that's distance and direction in a nutshell. Now let's see how these impact factors produce golf's most common mishits. Better still, you will find out how to wipe these bad shots from your full-swing repertoire.

Slicing

You may think there are dozens of reasons why the ball slices. Not true. There is actually only one root cause of the slice: an open clubface at impact. By this I mean the clubface points to the right of the path of the clubhead. For example, if the clubhead tracks straight down the target line through impact and the clubface points right of the target, the ball will pick up left-to-right sidespin from contact with the angled clubface. And sidespin is what makes the ball curve in the air.

But what causes the clubface to be open at impact? This is where the analysis can get a bit thick, so let's focus on two areas that plague most of the slicing population. The first culprit is a "weak" grip, where the hands are turned too far to the left on the handle at address. With this grip, when the hands are pulled into their natural positions by centrifugal force on the downswing, as discussed in "The Grip," the clubface flares open, resulting in a shot that spins off to the right.

The simple truth is that many slicers could straighten out their ball flight with a slight adjustment to their grip. They simply need to rotate their hands farther to the right on the handle, seeing about three knuckles on the left hand at address, and to make sure they hold the grip in their fingers, not their palms. With a better grip, the clubface will square up through impact and shot shape will improve dramatically.

The other major contributor to the slice is a failure to rotate the club through impact. Consider this: In a relaxed, rhythmic swing, the arms naturally release the club, the right forearm rotating over the left through the hitting area and therefore

Why Your Driver Slices Most

Left-to-right sidespin causes the ball to slice; backspin causes it to rise. In most shots, these opposing forces battle it out in the air. As a rule, the lower the loft on the club being used, the less backspin is imparted on the ball, which lets sidespin win the battle. This is why your driver slices worse than any other club in your bag: It has the least loft and imparts the most true sidespin on the ball.

closing the clubface. Unfortunately, many slicers have excessive hand and arm tension, which retards this rotation and leaves the clubface wide open at impact.

To promote a proper release, slicers need to soften their hands and arms, starting with a lighter grip, and let the swinging force of the clubhead turn the right forearm over the left. There's no need to strangle the club to prepare for impact; your body will naturally increase grip pressure to absorb the hit. Remember, a well-timed release will happen automatically—if you stay relaxed and simply let it.

Tense arms fail to rotate through impact, leaving the clubface open.

Without tension, the arms rotate and close the face.

BEST TIP: *Turn Your Back on a Slice*

Here's a drill to help you feel a full release. Take your address with a mid-iron, then shift your feet 90 degrees to your right, putting your back to the target and the ball off your left side. Hit some balls from this awkward position, half-swings at first. Since the swing can't extend much down the line, your arms are forced to release—right forearm rotating over left—promoting a closed clubface and right-to-left ball flight. After several swings, go back to your normal stance and try to feel the release.

—Rick McCord, *GOLF Magazine* Top 100 Teacher

Hooking

Since the slice and the hook send the ball in opposite directions, it makes sense that they stem from opposite faults. In fact, take everything just said about the slice and turn it the other way and there you have the hook, starting with a closed clubface at impact, which causes the ball to spin from right to left off the clubface and curve to the left.

Again, there are many ways to arrive at impact with a closed clubface, but we'll concentrate on two: a "strong" grip, with the hands turned too far to the right on the handle; and an early release, the hands and arms rotating prematurely on the downswing. If the hands start out in a strong position on the club, the force of the downswing will roll the clubface closed by impact, as the hands seek out their natural positions.

To correct a strong grip, simply turn the hands farther to the left on the handle at address, with the back of the left hand pointing more toward the target and the thumbs more on top of the handle. This will delay the closing rotation of the clubface on the downswing until after impact and thereby produce a straighter ball flight.

Clearly, a strong grip goes hand in hand with an early release, or excessive hand and arm rotation

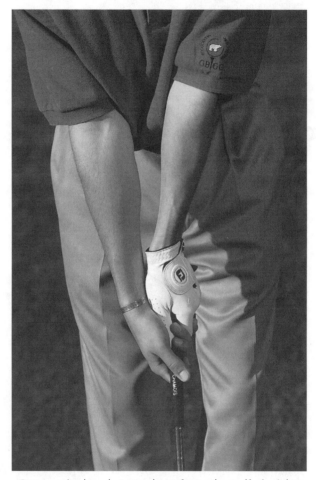

Strong grip: hands turned too far to the golfer's right.

A neutral grip helps keep the clubface square.

before impact. Players who hook tend to create too much rotation with a quick, overactive right hand at the start of the downswing. Focus on letting the lower body start the downswing, keeping the right hand and arm relaxed and passive. Don't forget,

> **BEST TIP: Swing an Inverted Club**
>
> To tame an overactive right hand and arm, turn your driver upside down, grip it around the hosel, and make some practice swings. Try to position the "swoosh" of the swing immediately after the spot where impact would be made. This trains you to save the fast point in your swing for the moment of impact.
>
> —Mike Lopuszynski, *GOLF Magazine*
> Top 100 Teacher

the release should happen by itself; allow the momentum of the clubhead to create the rotation.

Pulling

Like the hook, a pulled shot flies wide left of the target. The difference is the hook curves left, while the pull starts left and flies straight on that line. This type of ball flight tells us two things about impact: First, the swing path cut across the target line from out to in, producing a shot that starts left; and second, the clubface was square to the path, as the ball did not curve in the air.

We should note here that although path and clubface angle combine to determine the direction of every shot, one usually has more influence than the other, based on the loft of the club being used.

Since loft creates backspin and backspin counters the effect of sidespin, the more lofted the club, the less sidespin will affect the shape of the shot. As a result, direction in the more lofted clubs comes more from swing path than clubface angle. Conversely, the less lofted clubs impart relatively little backspin and therefore are more affected by the sidespin imparted by an open or closed clubface. This is why you can pull a 9-iron and slice a driver with the same swing and impact positions.

> ### When Face Matters More
>
> On full swings, swing path *primarily* determines a shot's starting direction, but it's actually a combination of path and clubface angle at impact. The slower the swing, the bigger the influence from clubface angle, as there's less forward propulsion. In fact, on the shortest shots—chips and putts—the starting direction is almost entirely determined by face angle at impact. With these shots, the ball simply deflects off the clubface in whatever direction it's facing.

Perhaps the two most common reasons for the pull are playing the ball too far forward in the stance and swinging "over the top" on the downswing. With the ball way up in the stance, the arms are forced to reach forward at address, which shifts the shoulders left, or "open" to the target. Since the arms tend to swing the club in the same direction that the shoulders are aligned, the swing path will tend to be out to in and the ball will start left.

Swinging over the top often leads to a pulled shot.

Let the lower body lead the downswing to keep the club inside.

First, check to make sure the ball is positioned correctly, and never farther forward than the left heel. It's also a good idea to confirm that your shoulders are not simply open to the target, as that alone could result in a yanked shot to the left. Check shoulder alignment by holding a club across your shoulders and seeing where it points.

Swinging over the top refers to the path of the clubhead on the downswing being over the top of, or steeper than, the path taken on the backswing. This often is caused by starting the downswing with the arms and shoulders, instead of the lower body, and therefore throwing the clubhead out of its natural inside path.

BEST TIP: For the Heel of It

Setting up with the ball off the heel of the clubface encourages an in-to-out swing path through impact, as you feel like you have to reroute the club closer to your body to find the center of the clubface. This is a great visual cue for correcting the out-to-in swing path that produces pulls and slices. In fact, look carefully and you'll notice many Tour players address the ball off the heel. Try it and see if your shots straighten out.

—Jim Flick, *GOLF Magazine*
Master Teaching Professional

Fixing an over-the-top downswing requires special attention to sequence of motion at the change of direction. Focus on letting the downswing occur from the ground up, keeping your back turned to the target and your torso coiled until the lower body pulls them into action. This will drop the club onto the desirable inside path to the ball.

Pushing

Often confused with its more popular cousin, the slice, the push is a shot that starts and flies straight right of the target. There is no midair curvature, which is what distinguishes it from the slice. Similar to the pulled shot, the push results from a swing path that cuts across the target line, in this case from in to out.

Two leading causes of the push are playing the ball too far back in the stance and sliding the hips too aggressively toward the target on the downswing. With the ball well back, the shoulders are pulled into a "closed" position, aligned at or right of the target, and the swing will tend to be in to out. Also, a back ball position doesn't give the clubhead enough time to start tracking down the target line by impact; in effect, contact is made too early in the swing. As a result, the ball is sent out to the right.

When the hips slide out in front, the typical result is a push.

To get rid of this problem, simply keep tabs on your
ball position, making sure it never creeps into the
back half of your stance or even near the middle
with your longer clubs.

As for the hip slide toward the target on the
downswing, this is the result of a good thing taken
too far. The hips *should* move toward the target as
you swing down, but when they slide too far, the
upper body must hang back to maintain balance,
which drops the clubhead back behind the right
hip. From there, the swing path cannot get back on

Think "shift, then turn" to calm overactive hips.

the target line by impact and the ball is pushed directly to the right.

To contain this lateral move, simply reorder your aggressiveness. Instead of sliding hard toward the target, try to make a slight lateral bump with the hips and then make an aggressive turn to the left. This will keep your upper body more stacked over your lower body and prevent the clubhead from getting stuck behind you.

BEST TIP: Slide Check

One good way to check how much your lower body is sliding on the downswing is to hit balls with the backs of your legs up against the back of a chair. Set up a folding chair facing directly away from you so that the top-back portion of the chair touches the backs of your thighs at address. Hit mid-iron shots with the chair in place. You'll be able to evaluate lateral movement in the lower body because you will feel your legs sliding along the back of the chair.

—Bill Moretti, *GOLF Magazine* Top 100 Teacher

Hitting Fat

While this blunder needs little introduction, the fat shot occurs when the club contacts the ground before the ball; in fact, the clubface often doesn't touch the ball at all, as a cushion of turf gets trapped between the two. The result, aside from a dead feeling in the hands at impact, is a dramatic reduction in clubhead speed and a miserably short ball flight.

Two of the more common causes of the fat shot are hunching over too much at address and dipping into the ball on the downswing. Let's start with address: If the upper body is slumped over and the

Being too hunched over at address often leads to heavy contact.

Get in a posture that will let your arms fully extend into the ball.

BEST TIP: The Light Touch

To ensure solid contact, your body posture must stay constant from setup through impact. To check this, take your normal address with a 5-iron, then stand the club vertically on its toe and hold it with just the index finger of your left hand. Practice swinging your right arm back and down, concentrating on keeping the club vertical and the pressure from your finger consistent (see photo at right). If you can do that, you're maintaining your address posture.

—Bruce Hamilton, *GOLF Magazine*
Top 100 Teacher

---

legs straight in the setup, the arms tend to "get lazy" and bend at the elbows. Then, when centrifugal force straightens the arms on the downswing, the true radius of the swing is realized and the swing lever becomes longer than it was at address. As a result, the clubhead bottoms out into the ground before reaching the ball.

To combat this posture problem, make sure you set up with a lively flex in your knees and that your left arm is fairly straight, although not rigid. You want to feel like you're swinging the club more around your body than up and down, giving centrifugal force a chance to fully extend your

arms and fire the clubhead into the back of the
ball.

The other major cause, dipping down into impact, often occurs as a desperate recovery for a lift-

ing action made on the backswing. Problem is, if you dip down a hair more than you lifted up, which is often the case, the clubhead will dive into the ground behind the ball. Again, a good setup goes a long way toward fixing this fault, as good posture is easier to maintain than poor posture.

Get into a relaxed, athletic position at address, then focus on winding your body over your right leg and then letting it unwind over your left leg, staying at the same height throughout. Maintaining the flex in your knees and the forward tilt of your spine through impact is the key to consistently returning the clubhead to the ball. If these critical angles are compromised, contact becomes a game of chance.

Popping Up

Pop-ups occur mostly on teed shots, especially driver shots, as they are caused by the clubhead glancing the ball on a steep descent and making contact on the very top portion of the clubface. Most pop-ups result from the player lunging toward the target with his upper body on the downswing and therefore having to drop the club steeply to get it back to the ball.

The ball flight of a pop-up is not only high but also very short, making it not exactly the most playable card in the deck. The height comes from the steep angle of approach, with the clubhead

Lunging the upper body forward causes pop-ups off the tee.

Keep your head behind the ball for a shallow approach.

grazing the ball on its way to the ground, thereby imparting a tremendous amount of backspin. This glancing contact transfers little energy from the clubhead to the ball, producing a shot without much forward momentum.

The steep swings that produce pop-ups are characterized by an up-and-down chopping motion with the arms. The best way to flatten out a steep swing is to add body turn. Since the shoulders move on a more horizontal plane than the arms, focusing on turning the shoulders leads to a shallower approach into the ball. But in order to trust that you'll make solid contact with a shallow approach, you must keep your head and upper body behind the ball through impact. That will correct the body lunge.

BEST TIP: Swing Uphill for Solid Contact

To learn to deliver the clubhead solidly at impact, practice hitting mid-iron shots from an uphill lie. The slope forces you to swing under and through the ball, which you can accomplish only by lowering your right shoulder. Hitting from an upslope also provides instant feedback: If the right shoulder stays high, a common mistake, the club will chop down into the hill. Think about swinging the clubhead up the slope rather than into it.

—Dana Rader, *GOLF Magazine* Top 100 Teacher

Hitting Thin

Flush shots occur when the clubface contacts the bottom half of the ball, except with the driver, when impact is more toward the middle. However, on most shots when the face meets the ball at or near its equator, you experience thin contact and a hollow feel that reverberates up the shaft and into your hands. The result is a line-drive trajectory and minimal backspin. However, the thin shot does approximate the distance of a well-struck shot, as the clubhead still meets the ball at full speed.

As with the fat shot, thin contact can be traced back to the setup. The player who overflexes his knees tends to set his spine too upright and is therefore asking for thin shots. Such posture promotes a very shallow, rounded swing plane, with the clubhead skimming the ground through impact. While this can be a beneficial swing shape for tee shots, it does not lead to pure strikes with the rest of the clubs.

Is It Fat or Thin?

It's commonly called a "drop-kick" when the clubhead hits the ground and ricochets into the ball. I suppose it qualifies as a fat shot, because the clubhead bottoms out into the ground, but it certainly feels thin, as contact occurs high on the ball. For advice on how to avoid this ugly mishit, see the discussion on reverse weight shift under "Hitting Thin," as most drop-kicks can be traced back to that fault.

If the weight moves left going back, it will fall right coming down.

To promote good posture, make sure you tilt your upper body first when taking your address, then flex your knees slightly to balance your weight on your insteps. Flexing the knees first leads to excessive flex and therefore a more upright spine, as posture is a balance of the two.

Another common cause of thin shots is the reverse weight shift, where the body weight moves to the left foot on the backswing and the right foot on

Loading onto your right side sets up a shift back to the target.

the downswing. When the weight shifts away from the target at impact, the left shoulder tilts upward, which starts the clubhead swinging upward to soon, leading to contact high on the ball. The thinner the contact, meaning higher on the ball, the lower and shorter the ball flight.

The key to combating a reverse weight shift is loading your body weight onto your right foot going back, led by a wide extension of the arms away

> ### BEST TIP: Practice in a Fairway Bunker
>
> Because of the lack of solid footing, hitting balls from a fairway bunker is a great way to promote proper weight movement. If you make a reverse weight shift in a bunker, you're likely to lose your balance. Hitting from sand teaches you to keep the lower body quiet, letting your weight transfer naturally to your rear foot going back and to your front foot coming down. It will also help improve the tempo of your swing.
>
> —Todd Sones, *GOLF Magazine* Top 100 Teacher

from the ball. If you can load up going back, your weight will naturally transfer to your left foot coming down. With your weight driving forward, you set up the descending angle of approach necessary to pinch the ball off the ground.

Topping

Hitting thin shots is bad enough, but topping the ball may be the golfer's most embarrassing miss. A topped shot is essentially a shot hit so thinly that the leading edge of the clubface contacts the ball above its equator, causing the ball to compress into the ground and dribble only a short distance.

The topped shot can have a devastating effect on the golfer's psyche. For one, topping is associated with beginners, who lift their heads anxiously in an effort to see where the ball is going. The problem is that lifting your head means lifting the arc of your swing as well, which pulls the clubhead well off the ground at impact.

Experienced golfers sometimes still make the mistake of peeking too soon, but more likely their topped shots come from the same faults that cause thin shots, only exaggerated. They make such a severe reverse weight shift and put so much weight on their rear leg at impact that the rising arc of the clubhead nearly misses the ball completely.

When the weight transfer problem is this dramatic, it's a good idea to set extra weight on the rear foot at address. This presets the loading action normally performed on the backswing and promotes a forward shift on the downswing, driving the body through the shot.

Topping can also result from a premature unhinging of the wrists, or scooping action, on the downswing, often caused by an overactive right hand. If this occurs and the clubhead passes the hands before impact, the swing arc is rising and contact will be high on the ball—slightly high means a thin shot, higher means a topped shot.

> ## BEST TIP: Get to Your Front Foot
>
> Topping often results from hanging back on your right side. Here's a good way to find out if your weight is getting back to your left foot by impact. Tee a ball a half inch off the ground and hit it with a 5-iron. But here's the kicker: Take a divot after impact without disturbing the tee. To hit a teed ball solidly and then take a divot, your weight has to be transferred to your front foot, with your upper body well into its forward rotation.
>
> —Craig Shankland, *GOLF Magazine*
> Top 100 Teacher

Shanking

Nothing strikes fear in the hearts of golfers like the shank, golf's mysterious malady. It occurs when the hosel of the club, instead of the clubface, contacts the ball and sends it darting off to the right. Many players won't even utter the word "shank" on the golf course out of fear that it might somehow bring on a bout of these alarming mishits.

But they're only as mysterious as you make them. The shank only rears its ugly head when the hosel of the clubhead moves closer to the ball at impact than it was at address. The problem could be that you're simply standing too close to the ball and your arms reroute the club during the swing into a less cramped

If your weight goes to your toes, you're asking for a shank.

To conquer the shanks, keep your weight toward your heels and your arms relaxed.

position. But most shanks happen for one of two rea-sons: Either the arms tense up and pull out away from the body on the downswing or the upper body leans toward the ball. Both can send the shot hard right.

Treating a case of the shanks has to start in the mind. After you hit one, let it go and approach the next shot with a positive and confident attitude— easy to say, tough to do. At address, make sure your hands are set a comfortable distance from your thighs, about the width of your hand, giving your arms room to swing back. As for the swing, which tends to become a short, tense swipe after a few shanks, take some deep, calming breaths and focus on keeping your weight toward your heels from setup to finish and making a smooth swing, with the arms staying soft through impact. Remember, every new swing is a chance to do something spectacular.

BEST TIP: Shank Cure

Place two balls side by side on the ground, about an inch apart. Address the ball that's far-ther from you, then swing and try to hit the near ball. If you can consistently hit the near ball, you're pulling the club closer to you dur-ing the swing—the opposite of a shank swing— and putting your move back on track.

—Martin Hall, *GOLF Magazine*
Master Teaching Professional

Practice

To many golfers, "practice" is a dirty word. They'd rather say "hitting balls" or "going to the range," which says a lot about how slack and unstructured their practice habits are. I'm not going to start preaching here, but if you see the practice tee as a place where you blow off some steam or have long-drive contests with your buddies, fine; just don't expect it to help your golf game. Hitting balls may be enjoyable, but you need to have a purpose to make it productive.

For starters, realize that you can change your golf swing. You can learn to hit the ball longer, straighter, higher—whatever you like. Sure, some faults are tougher to overcome than others, but if you know where you want to improve and implement a plan, how well you progress is up to you.

Practice hard and you may quickly see dramatic improvement; take it slowly and you'll have to wait. But you have to believe it will come along. Your efforts will be rewarded.

Practicing and Playing

You may find this hard to believe, but some golfers actually like to practice. They like the feeling of grooving their swing during long hours on the practice tee, finding the secret "in the dirt," as Ben Hogan used to say. Others would opt for a root canal over a bucket of balls. Instead, they spend their golf time on the course, engaged in battles with Old Man Par.

Most golfers fall into the latter group, claiming to have neither the time nor the motivation for the practice tee. In many cases, the real culprit is a lack of structure to their practice sessions. Twenty minutes of ball-beating, the last fifteen with the driver, and they start getting bored or tired, wondering why they're not playing golf. They're right to call these sessions meaningless, as practice without a purpose is simply time wasted.

First, understand that practicing and playing golf are totally different activities. In practice, you work on the mechanics of the swing, trying to achieve certain positions or moves. On the course, the game changes, the object is to forget about mechanics and focus on hitting targets. Sure, you're using the swing you've grooved on the practice tee, but most golfers play their best when they put aside thoughts of swing technique.

The good news is, you can learn things on the golf course—in fact, you need to. Since there is often no correlation between how well you perform on the range and how well you play, you need to keep track of where your game falters on the course. Are poor drives leading to double bogeys? Are you missing all your approaches to one side? Do you have trouble getting out of the rough? These are the types of questions you need to ask yourself, and the answers can only come from a careful analysis of your rounds.

If you watch the pros at Tour events, they often spend more time on the range after they play than before. They know that the intensity of playing "live" shots, having one swing to pull them off, exposes your weaknesses and shows how much you trust your swing. Heading to the range right after the round, when the highs and lows are still fresh in your mind, leads to a more focused, productive practice session.

You should also take advantage of practicing on the course whenever you can. The practice tee doesn't offer all the challenges of a round of golf, such as driving between tight treelines, playing from uneven lies, and hitting out of deep rough.

This is one reason to play an occasional round by yourself when the course isn't busy: You can play an extra ball or two from these situations to familiarize yourself with the strategy required.

BEST TIP: *Rehearsal Swings*

Think of practice swings on the course as "dress rehearsals" for the shot at hand. To accomplish this, you must have a clear image of the shot, with consideration for the lie of the ball, the overall terrain, and the distance and trajectory. Then pick a specific object on the ground, such as a broken tee or a dandelion, and try to strike it with your practice swing. This will focus your attention and lead to an accelerating, descending blow, just as you want in your actual swing.

—Eddie Merrins, *GOLF Magazine*
Top 100 Teacher

Home on the Range

The practice tee is the ideal spot for practicing or warming up before a round. Unfortunately, many golfers think these activities are one and the same. Truth is, practicing involves working on your technique, while warming up is simply a way of getting your golf muscles ready to play.

As for practicing, every session should begin with a plan. What has lead you to the practice tee? What do you hope to accomplish? Too many amateurs toil away, beating balls with blind fury, without thinking much about what they're doing. It's not enough to just put in the practice time; you have to take a critical look at where you need improvement, and then map out a plan to get there, including when to practice and what clubs, shots, or practice drills to work on.

Here are a few hints for getting started. Begin each practice session at the putting green. Stroke some short putts, then some lag putts, and hit a handful of chips and pitches before heading to the range. You might ask, "Why bother with the small stuff?" Because even the shortest putt is the golf swing in miniature—fewer moving parts but the same objective. It makes sense to start simple, where the targets are easier to hit and the swing is less complicated, and to build on the motion as you go.

Once you get to the practice tee, follow the same philosophy as above, starting with the short irons and gradually working your way up to the longer clubs. Whatever you're hitting, it's critical to pick a target for each shot, using range flags or target greens if possible, or at least a landmark on the horizon. Also, lay clubs on the ground as alignment guides,

Even short putts are the golf swing in miniature.

Use clubs on the ground to develop good alignment habits.

one at your toes and another just outside the ball, to make sure you're aimed where you think you are. Get into the habit of structuring your sessions.

Fine-Tuning

Most golfers practice to become more consistent when they play, to fine-tune what they have, not to make major swing changes. That being the case, the key is to simulate on-course situations as much as possible. To do this, imagine the confines of a fairway or the surface of a green and take aim on every swing. Use the treelines or boundary fences on the range as obstacles and play shots from different lies, even hitting out of a divot hole now and then. Also, change targets frequently, just as you do on the course.

When you have some time, do yourself a favor and find out how far you hit each club. Hit ten balls with each club in your bag, perhaps splitting it over two sessions, and figure out the average carry for each. Don't take the best shot with each—estimate the *average*. Too many golfers make club selections based on the maximum yardage they can stretch out of a given club. They think they can reproduce that distance every day. Avoid one of the biggest playing faults among amateurs by establishing a realistic distance for each club.

Practice Trajectory

Every round of golf presents situations where you need to hit a shot either over or under an intervening obstacle, such as a tree limb. Although it's tough to convince yourself to spend valuable range balls on trouble shots, you should spend a few minutes every so often trying to control trajectory. Practice high and low shots, as well as draws and fades—you'll need them all sooner than you're willing to admit.

Another valuable use of practice time is working on your tempo. Extended practice sessions, provided you aren't just blistering drive after drive, loosen your muscles and groove good rhythm. When the clubhead starts to feel heavy and you can sense the pull of centrifugal force during the swing, your muscles are warm and performing at their best. Try to internalize this feeling of relaxed power and recall it on the golf course.

You should also hit some shots going through your entire preshot routine, starting from behind the ball just as you should on the course. This can be tedious, so work out a system you can faithfully adhere to. Dr. Richard Coop, *GOLF Magazine*'s Mental Game Consultant, recommends performing the preshot routine before every fifth shot— that's about all most golfers have patience for.

Finally, don't try to be somebody you're not when you practice. If you get bored after thirty minutes, go back to the putting green for a while,

On the range, practice your preshot routine, too.

or take a short break. The trick is to make each shot count: If you're practicing with a friend, play a game of closest to the pin; if you're alone, put yourself on the last hole of the U.S. Open. When your mind wanders elsewhere, you're no longer practicing effectively. Come back another day.

> ### *BEST TIP: Groove Good Tempo*
>
> If your swing tends to get fast, especially on the range, hit balls with the image of a good finish position in your mind: arms and club high, chest facing the target, weight on the outside of the front foot. As you swing, hold on to this image and try to match it. You'll start thinking about swinging the club instead of hitting the ball, and as a result, you'll slow down and gain control.
>
> —Johnny Myers, *GOLF Magazine*
> Top 100 Teacher

Making Changes

Some trips to the practice tee are made out of necessity. Every golfer's swing slips off track now and then, requiring critical attention. The range is the perfect place—the only place—to work on swing mechanics. Playing golf with your mind cluttered with mechanical thoughts, such as swing plane or weight shift, is a recipe for frustration. The body works best when the mind stays out of its way. That means trusting your mechanics.

There are a couple of viable ways to improve your swing mechanics. First, you can seek the help of a PGA professional, whose experience and expertise can put you on the right path. It may cost you a few bucks, but in time you will almost certainly improve. Or, you can go it alone, using the lessons you read in books and magazines. This is a trickier proposition, as the golf swing can be deceptive—you aren't always doing what you think you're doing. That's why it's a good idea to periodically record your swing on video and review it as objectively as possible.

When working on a specific part of your swing, such as your takeaway or your position at the top, isolate your thinking to that area. This is one time when ball flight doesn't really matter; the key is grooving the proper sensation and getting it on video for later analysis. It's also advisable to make shorter, slower swings when changing your technique, as your body will more easily incorporate the changes, and to use clubs with which you're most comfortable—say, a 7-iron instead of a driver.

The problem with focusing on one particular area is that the golf swing is a single flowing motion. Sure, there are swing positions and checkpoints along the way, but motion is the glue that holds them all together. To make sure you never lose sight of this, always intersperse normal swings between any drills or modified swings you're working on. And if things ever get real ugly, make some swings, even half-swings, thinking only about producing smooth tempo back and through.

When making a swing change, focus your work in one area.

Warming Up

If you have the luxury of hitting balls before you play, by all means do it. But keep in mind that your objective is to ready your body for golf, not to practice. Tinkering with your swing before you play leads to mechanical thoughts on the course, and that spells trouble: confusion in your head, tension in your body, and big numbers on the scorecard.

The warm-up, like the practice session, should start on the putting green, where you can regain a feel for the basic golf stroke and for aiming at targets.

Playing Well? Take a Lesson

It makes perfect sense that the only time most golfers pay a visit to their local pro is when their game has left them. But consider taking a lesson when your swing feels right and you're hitting the ball the way you like. It's a good idea to have your pro see how your "A" game looks, even get it on video to check against that other swing that surfaces now and then. This is precisely what the Tour players do with their teachers.

From there, a few chips or pitches are useful, if time permits. Most golfers are eager to get to the practice tee, which is where you really need to discipline yourself. As tempting as it is to grab a full bucket of balls and start whacking them into outer space, stick to a simple plan, such as the following:

• Stretch your big rotational muscles. Standing up straight, hold a club across your back and practice turning to your right, then your left. Slowly assume your golf posture as you turn, tilting your upper body forward and flexing your knees.

• Rehearse the swinging motion. Take two clubs in a baseball grip and swing them back and through several times, increasing speed as you go. The extra weight will get the blood pumping to your hands, wrists, and arms.

• Start with half-wedge shots. Focus on smooth tempo and crisp contact, then hit some full shots with your wedge or another short iron.

BEST TIP: *How to Use Video*

Video is an indispensable tool in monitoring the golf swing. Have a friend film your swing from three angles: face-on (facing your chest), down-target (target in the background), and rear view (facing your back). To ensure consistency from session to session, shoot from the same exact perspective every time: From face-on and rear view, set the camera in line with the leading edge of the clubface; from down-target, align the camera halfway between the stance and the ball. Video sessions are always revealing—even with the world's best players.

—Robert Baker, *GOLF Magazine*
Master Teaching Professional

Pick a target for each shot and try to make all your actions relaxed and unhurried. Tension is reflected in every swing.

- Hit a handful of mid-irons. Again your focus should be establishing good rhythm and zeroing in on a target. If you've hit more than fifteen shots at this point, slow down—the worst thing you can do now is slip into rapid-fire mode.

- Play a few tee shots. Notice I didn't say "launch" or "pound" or "rip." Many amateurs kick their swing speed up a notch when they pull out the big stick. Remember why you're there: to warm up your muscles, not test their limits.

- Cool down with a wedge. By now you're ready to go, but you don't want to head off to the first tee with an aggressive mind-set. Go back to the wedge and pitch a few balls to a very demanding target, such as a range flag or even a single ball.

- Roll a few more. If you still have time to kill, stroke some short putts. Don't worry if you make or miss them, just enjoy the smooth motion that warm muscles produce. The critical point is not to waste your warm-up session by sitting idle until it's time to go. Now you're ready to play some golf.